Wild Soul

Also by Susan Marshall

Fiction

The Adira Cazon Literary Mystery Series:
Adira and the Dark Horse

Poetry

Bare Spirit: The Selected Poems of Susan Marshall

Plays

The Theatre Playscapes series:
Fleur of Yesterday
All the Hope We Carry

Single, Full-length Plays:
Indigo's Haven
Broken World

Essays & Articles

Theatre Playscapes: A New Theatrical Style
Theatre Playscapes of Hope

Contemporary Classical Winter Poetry

Wild Soul

Susan Marshall

For the Wild Soul and its journeys.

Published in Australia in 2024 by
Story Playscapes
Victoria, Australia
ABN 62197863313

publications@storyplayscapes.com
www.storyplayscapes.com

Copyright © Susan Marshall, 2025

All rights reserved. Apart from any fair dealing for the purposes of private study, research, criticism or review as permitted under the Copyright Act, no part of this publication may be translated, adapted, performed, reproduced, stored in a retrieval system or transmitted in any forms by any means, electronic, mechanical, photocopying, recording or otherwise, without the written permission of the publisher.

This book is a work of fiction. The names, characters, places and events are products of the author's imagination and any resemblance to actual persons or events, past or present, is entirely coincidental.

A catalogue record for this book is available from the National Library of Australia

Title:	Wild Soul: Contemporary Classical Winter Poetry
Author:	Susan Marshall
Compiled by:	Susan Marshall
Book Designer:	Ryan Marshall
ISBN:	9780645404180
Subjects:	Poetry / Australian & Oceanian
	Fiction / Visionary & Metaphysical
	Fiction / Romance / General

Produced by Story Playscapes
Written by Susan Marshall
Compiled by Susan Marshall
Book design, illustration and photography by Ryan Marshall

All images and text are Copyright © Story Playscapes

The opinions expressed in this publication are those of the author and do not necessarily reflect those of the views of Story Playscapes. While all reasonable checks have been made to ensure the accuracy of statements and advice, no responsibility can be accepted for errors, omissions or representations, express or implied. The author and Story Playscapes do not, under any circumstance, accept any responsibility or loss occasioned to any person acting or refraining from action as a result of material in this publication.

Warning: This book contains mature content, including adult themes and sexual references. It is not intended to be read by any persons under 18 years of age.

Contents

8	Wild Woman Soul
12	O Sweet Florence, Unearth My Soul
14	Winter Solstice's Secret
16	Dark Storm Melody
20	Lost Flame of Love
24	Silent Flight
26	Wild Artist's Soul
28	Stirring her Storm
30	Harboured Love
32	Your Voice Hides
34	Cold Frost, Quieten my Heart
36	Beats of Wander
38	Tiny, Soulful Dancer
42	Love's Wild Silhouette
44	Stoic Solitude
48	Wild Alive
52	Hold onto My Fire Heart
54	A Shelter for the Soul
56	Wild Love
58	Spirit of the Light
60	Free Soul
62	Rise of the Daffodil
64	Kiss Me with Clear Sight
	Sonnets
66	I
67	II
68	III
69	IV
70	V
71	VI
72	VII
73	VIII
74	About the Author
77	Acknowledgements
78	About the Book Designer
78	About Story Playscapes

Wild Woman Soul

My wild soul drifts,
a smoky white haze,
alighting teal blue tint
across the hill tops.
I sit cross legged,
absorbing the stark
energy of winter white.

Thatched roofs glow
in the near distance,
like snowy mountain peeks
in the heart of winter.
Locked doors forbid
soul's sensual growth
in the alluring air outside.

Outside in the open,
rebelling against rule,
allured by the atmosphere.
White whispers of mist
journey around my torso
and deeply into my lungs,
arousing my anticipation.

Raw and ready, I step,
across the rocky ridge.
Exhaling a large breath,
I expel the wild mist.
It circles the rough rocks,
tossing them into the air,
stacking them solidly.

A hut with no walls,
shaped by my sensuality.
My wild woman soul,
unlocked and unafraid,
alight in the alluring air.

Hot hours etch their presence
like short, seductive breaths.
Ascending through open sky roof,
wrapped by a red raw sky,
I embrace the sensual flame.

Arms outstretched and open,
I readily rise into time's passion.
Skin kissing fragmentary sparks
of the day's lingering, bare blaze.
Shades of evescape do seep through
the fine pores of time's canvas,
forming a pool of passion
that floods my soaring soul.

A gentle touch tingles my soul,
unwinding a trail of deep desire.
Closing my eyes, I caress
time's burning, raw atmosphere.

Harnessing winter's energy, I drift,
my free, wild woman's soul,
alight with day's deep desires.
Surrendering a hot heat trail,
a steamy, sultry fume across eve.

O Sweet Florence, Unearth My Soul

O sweet Florence, majestic city,
unearth my soul in purity.
Bless my eyes with vision
of the Duomo's graciousness.

Architrave of pietra serena,
chiseled by gifted hands.
Share your entablature's voice
of life amongst your people.

Upon the tiled roof of the Duomo,
my soul soars high above me.
Spanning its wings like a bird,
flying over the city's houses.

A soul that reaches for life,
unravelled across the cobble.
Stones that carry my artistry
towards the market stalls.

Fellow artists span their wings
of heritage beauty in design.
Giving fuel to my flight
of creative imagination.

My tapestry bag sings in the rain,
as I continue to trek across
the beautiful Point Vecchio,
agleam with its survival tales.

Tales that shed tears in my heart,
as I consider life's grace.
Souls that nourished our world,
saving Point Vecchio's life.

Bare foot on Arno River's bank,
I scratch wet dirt for sediment.
Small rocks and clumps of dirt,
I throw up high into the sky.

Words scroll across dark clouds,
revitalising my will to be.
A bric-a-brac of feelings,
nurtured deeply within me.

Words that awaken my soul,
a Renaissance of artistry.
Elated with contentment,
my creative energy flows.

Winter Solstice's Secret

Feast's flame sparks incessantly,
devouring the last day of harvest.
A decadent display of bonfire
across the aged green of gather.
Holding winter solstice's secret,
I dare to unleash my desire
in night's lingering last hour.

Bare naked beneath robes,
gifted to me by your Grace.
Coated with rich red rubies
that could buy a small hut
or nourish a starving soul,
I gasp with guilt's breath.

Revived by winter's blast,
lying back in farm's hay,
pecked at by wealthy hens.
Gathering minuscule seeds,
untying the ruby robe,
scattering scarce seeds on
my shaking, bare breasts.

Our bonfire burns brightly,
alighting our hot harvest.
Scarce seeds of winter's heat,
as its first dawn inflames.
Sprouting into a plant
that roots within my soul.
Shooting into magnolias
of purity and nobility.

My deep magnolia soul,
a precious, pure forest,
that unwinds its unruly path
before your baffled gaze.

Take me in your arms,
I gift myself to you, my Grace.
I may be poor but mighty wise.
Subdue your worn weapons,
immerse yourself in peace.

Your hunger teems down,
devouring me with kisses
that rain across my stomach
and stir my supple loins.
I arch my allured back,
showering your starving soul
with pure magnolia petals.

As the glow of winter morning,
sheds its light upon you skin,
you gather my magnolia bouquet,
cradling me in your calmness.
Stepping out on gold grass,
you face my fellow people.

Holding me up high to light,
you bend down on bare knee.
Relinquishing your rage,
you lay down your sword
and promise a life of peace.

Dark Storm Melody

Burnt white piano keys,
alight beneath my finger tips.
A haunting, echoic melody,
as heavy as my breath
in this confined library.

The hour's bell tolls
like the weight of snow,
burying the world of sight.
Eternal time that passes,
forsaking heart's song.

The rose's petals shed
last breaths as they drift
away from stem's life,
falling in a pining pile.
Petals I clasp in palms,
savouring fading scent,
releasing them into air.

Petals afloat in melody,
bittersweet reds of love.
Circling centuries of books,
refreshing them with fragrance.
Books that shed their pages,
burdens of bleak days
when windows were black
from the soot of fire.

Outside the rain teems down,
setting windows aspark
with lightening's wild wrath.
My melody rises in dynamics,
saturated by storm's force
and unravelling a dark cloud.

A mass of time's grey burdens,
satiated by storm's noise.
My fingers press keys forcefully,
transforming rose petals into faces.
Spirits of family who glow
like the last light before storm.
Lingering life that sets sail
upon the decks of books.

Tales that stood the test
of one winter's fiery blaze
that devoured our home's heart,
myself the only survivor.
Too early was life lost,
shrouding my soul in a storm
that builds as eve darkens,
rising to my deep crescendo.

A sound that engulfs space,
like the thunderous storm,
falling from the dark cloud,
saturating my sad soul.

Soaked I am afloat,
across my sea of sadness,
joining my family at sail
towards lands that linger
with our beloved stories.

Lands once shared in light,
pages fuelling imagination,
free of the fierce flames,
lives burning with anticipation.
Souls to be carried safely
across storm's deep sorrows,
into the light of love
found in our story's pages.

Lost Flame of Love

Outside the wild wind howls,
its gusts tearing at my torso.
Beneath my bare skin is a carriage,
a tiny, tethered home that houses
my beating, burnt coal heart,
searching for its lost flame of love.

My weathered wooden rail legs
struggle to shift across the dirt.
They carry the great cargo
of love's hurt, lingering weight,
which smothers and restrains me.

For many days I have despaired
as dark and dusk crossed paths.
Blurring by on my steam train,
memories of our precious past
were fogged by frosty windows.

Your flame cannot be extinguished
as it lingers like a lantern in the dark.
It once clung tightly to my carriage,
guiding me safely across day's dares.
If only I could take those solo steps
across the wide abyss of our divide.

Our fight struck sharp swords
through our firm foundations.
You abandoned my carriage,
dividing our souls across tracks.

Left without your warmth for days,
a cold chill settled itself within me.
My steam train began to slow down,
unsure of its precise destination.
The air was persistently penetrated
by our stubborn, fuming silence.

I felt my steam shrink within,
coiling silently like a snake.
My soul, once bound to yours,
was lost and lingering in ...
our fading familiar.

Against my wooden rail legs,
my skirt billows in the breeze.
Its dramatic drapes tickle
my stark, very silent skin.
It is the one item that remains,
the skirt you stitched for me.
You traced the tight contours
of my body with your bare hands
as you fitted it to my frame.

A warmth stirs within me,
vibrating with vivid life,
sparking my aching abdomen
with lingering, lost love.
In your stark, silent absence,
your tender touch still ignites me.
If that is all I have left, it is enough.

The warmth builds to a heat
that kindles my steam engine.
I am ready to face our unknown,
to break our strange divide.
My burnt, coal heart is aflutter ...

Your lantern's light glows softly,
a mighty message in the night.
In silence, you have stayed here,
across our mad, raging abyss
as wide as my waiting arms stretch.

My steam engine propels forward,
carrying my weight of cargo,
towards my new destination.
It exists somewhere in your projection
of lantern aflame with love's hope.

Your light throbs with intensity,
as we meet at our unknown place.
I enclose you in a cloud of steam,
drawing you closer to my soul.
Rage abandoned in arousal,
our silent lips lock sensually.
My raw, racing heart pounds
as you sensually stroke my thigh.

Tearing at my nervous neckline,
I rip away ruefully at buttons,
releasing raw skin under blouse.
Dark steam parts my lips,
carrying the weight of our troubles.
Its rawness rises sharply,
evacuating my tight, tiny carriage.
Ascending night's air it beats,
a burnt coal heart revived.

Silent Flight

Distant bells chime with life
as the world ticks by time.
A voracious village empty
of nature's food to forage.

Her hut is harshly bare,
like her child's stomach.
Screaming in despair,
her cries bud feathers.

Feathers that span space,
soft and silent in flight.
She soars high in the sky,
sharp eyes peeling night.

An instinctive flyer is she,
aglow with night's gaze.
Her silent owl soul
at hunt in home range.

Starved and stark is she,
who lands on bare talons,
snapping twig and pellet
in the tension of time.

Silent Flight

The snow masks soil,
hiding heart's prey,
a desperate feast
for her growing child.

A scuttering sound stirs
tension in time's span.
Feet step fast and closer,
on the hunt for harvest.

Daring to dig quickly,
her talons tear at snow.
Fortune brings a field vole,
which she clasps in beak.

Two eyes flash in eve,
staring into her soul.
A gun glares its face,
marking her as prey.

Tense and tenacious,
she soars into the sky.
Near-missing the gunshot,
a mother has survived.

Wild Artist's Soul

Atop the city's tiled roof,
a wild artist's soul,
slandered with shards
of icy, cold accusation.

Feet bare and brazen,
hunted yet undetected.
Scratching amongst debris
for remnants of humanity.

Seeking beyond ash and twig,
digging deep into ideals.
New approaches to art,
a rebirth of antiquity.

Rain beats its blame of vanity,
awash within my budding soul.
My broken body crouches,
a solo entity, unable to grow.

Protecting all I have left,
my arms reach very high.
Shards of my battled sleeves
rip away, escaping slander.

Afloat they transform,
into tiny, pointed particles.
Free, wild roaming ideas,
artistry alive beyond storm.

My bare, beating arms
are buoys in the tidal waves.
I reach for my humanity
in burdening black night.

Wreckless water falls,
like thousands of tears
that befell the broken streets
over the last lingering days.

Across the stoned streets,
bonfires engulf new ideas.
Artistry lost in the blame
of rageful red, fiery flames.

I cry out in desperation,
seeking shelter from danger.
Soaked in the dark droplets
of righteous, teeming rain.

My saturated soul carries
the weight of humanity
that once adorned the streets
with new ideals of life.

I am a self lost at sea,
seeking a way to survive.
I yearn to discover *me*
in the raging red light.

Stirring her Storm

She exists in sands of time,
asway in stinging breeze.
Skirt pocket full of fevered
tears of her traumatic days.

Tears that estrange her storm,
hiding it from the glowing sun.
Depriving her of consolation
at the death of her beloved.

Her hour glass trickles slowly,
sifting through her memory.
Tiny granules of lost love
that pine away at her heart.

Her forgotten world fades,
shrinking away from light.
Dark curses her tears as stones
to throw at her broken soul.

Ornate broken wings,
hearts chipped away,
stones she glues to walls
of the home love shared.

Shifting through shadows,
she stirs her pending storm.
Her soul forms looming clouds
that float across the black.

Miniature, yet magnificent,
her soul storm unleashes
a wild blast of windy rain
of tears upon her cheeks.

The sand particles pile
into a muddy mound.
Memories she now feels
with her mending heart.

Harboured Love

Upon a brazen boulder of time
we stand worn and weathered
as love's boat abandons us.
Stranded on our harbour,
time ticking vehemently,
we meet each others' gazes.

Deep patterns of despair,
trek their firm journeys
across your golden pupils.
They wear away at your gaze,
darkening your desperation.

Dipping my bare brush
into your garish gold eyes,
I draw your dreams close.
They dance divinely within,
sparkling silhouettes alight.

Dark, shifting movements,
aglow with golden lights.
Their rhythm unravelling
life through my hands
and soft, bare brush.

The sky our stark canvas,
smeared with sparkly gold.
A new pathway of promise,
washing away your ache,
reviving your raw soul.

As silent as the shifting wind,
your silhouette is adrift,
sparkling alight with shine.
You set my spirit abreeze,
I merge with you and wander.

We are wrapped in our magic,
our bare spirits blending,
casting a ribbon of light,
that sets the shadows free
from our harboured love.

Your Voice Hides

Your voice hides like a dim
glow in the grey clouded sun.
A lingering echo in the blast
of blinding wind that weeps.

I chase your voice across grass,
wet with the drops of tears,
frosted with the fall of snow,
seeking you out of shadows.

The clouds clutter my head,
swirling with sorrow's storm.
I cry a million, longing tears,
missing the heat of your sun.

Your Voice Hides

In tall grass blades I lie,
in a lingering love memory,
feeling stalks stroke skin,
like your tender touch.

Your dim light radiates,
shifting storm clouds aside.
It shines freely on my skin
with the warmth of your love.

Your voice wind sweeps wildly,
abandoning storm's shadows.
Circling my lost, longing soul,
it echoes deeply in my heart.

Cold Frost, Quieten my Heart

Cold frost, quieten my heart,
that thumps ferociously like
the untamed snow storm
that left its mad mark
with piles of painful white.

Airy and icy, you linger,
like a frozen breath exhaled.
White particles through air
do collect and disperse
the debris of days passed.

Hours too long to attend,
rather blur out with the fog,
massed within my marred mind.
Clumpy thoughts clamber days,
bogged with the burden of time.

Feet deep in snow, saturated
by the world's heavy weight
as it takes tough grip of
my deep, buried soul.

An impasse, to trek ahead
and face the path untaken.
Her hand, always cold,
still leaves its imprint
upon my shaking palm.

Raw, righteous frost,
you are the breath of my beloved
who walked wildly with me
across the daring, icy days,
undeterred by sudden storms.

Reawaken the spirit within me,
to scatter its showers upon
the worn out, white ground
and shatter the storm of pain.

Buried beneath snow's burden
is the lingering light I seek.
Rays that raise her spirit
within day's devouring love.

Beats of Wander

The sun lingers, its heat warming
the depths of my hibernated soul.
Steps soak up the hues of day,
saturating my mind with ideas.
Unravelling my writer's heart
upon the scarce winter heat
of sharp, yet smooth rocks,
I begin to visualise anew.

Words are entering my mind again,
beginning beats of wander,
that set my wandering rhythm.

With such lightness I tread,
allowing myself to breathe and …
wonder.

A rejuvenation, to be out again,
enjoying our earth's company.
The gentle brush of a leaf
upon my shoulder as I pass.
The glorious, vibrant pinks of
magnolias in bloom.

The reassuring grounding
of my bare feet on earth.
Its reminder of existence
and its daily tread.

Peaceful, yet wakeful moments
begin to unravel
in my mind,
forming new buds
of ideas and stories.

A joy to let words enter
my open heart again.
To play with ideas gleaned
and express them on paper.
A simple brainstorm
or a word or sentence ...
emerging creativity.

It soothes my soul to listen
to the very beats of our world.
Connections with moments
linger within my heart,
sorting out their meanings,
their ways to be expressed.
I interpret their rhythms and
movements through my words.

A heart at peaceful rest,
out in the open and
at one with my wanders.
Hope soars within me
as I begin to reconnect
with my writer's heart again ...

Tiny, Soulful Dancer

A wrought iron gate opens,
creaking loudly in the quiet.
As I take some soft steps,
the snow-stormed ferns sway,
reaching out towards me as I pass,
like a welcome to …
a place I barely remember.

I know my memory is rusty,
like the archway which stands
tall and foreboding in the quiet.
It keeps a watchful eye on …
the visitor.
Is that what I am?

The front door looks worn out,
like my fighting, fatigued soul,
which wishes to find its place
amongst the aging, scattered
memories that fill the blank air.

Chipped bricks and leaning columns
leer at me like watchful soldiers,
guarding a monumental treasure.
Determination dares to fill me
and I push away the aged door,
my soul swinging with anxiety.

The giant glass table triggers
a dark cloak of coping:
fallen leaf fragments,
scraps I scattered upon the dirt,
hoping they would heal time.

Outside in the barren garden,
I once spoke to someone,
soothing their very soft hands.
I close my eyes and focus ...

I see a face as free as air,
abreeze amongst the aged wind.
A spiritual lightness that scatters
into a million fine fragments
that I yearn to seek and save,
to put the pieces back together.

Standing in the still space,
I gaze at the wallowing walls,
which carry the cargo of life
imprinted in their identity.
Music seeps from cracks,
breathing a bare melody
across time's lingering memory.
Faint and familiar, it lures me
towards the dainty dining table,
marked with the muddied
fingerprints of family life.

Precious tunes overcome me,
stirring my sad soul.
Music I melted into
as I held a small hand,
beating with brave life,
in mine ...

The music transforms momentarily,
scattering a child's soulful laughter
across the stark blankness.

Pitter-patter echoes
are acute in the silent moments.
Do I reach down and ...
pick you up?

You're not here.

Soul filled with love,
I sway and slide,
dancing with the divine,
tiny soulful dancer.
A sacred, loved spirit,
that takes its shape
in my broken, brave mind.

Love's Wild Silhouette

My soul darkens with despair
at our loss of love's freedom.
Your wide eyes reach for me,
willing me to rid of the shadows.
In danger, we estrange ourselves,
releasing our wild silhouettes
from our raw, hunted souls.

Our silhouettes haunt our hideaway,
energised by winter's cold blasts,
frosting our rooms as museums,
that display our love moments.
A love that we are devoted to,
as winter white is set aflame,
fuelling the strict, suited rage.
Our families mortal enemies,
forbidding our desired love,
determined to tear us apart.

In hiding our silence bleeds
through the walls of noise.
It clashes with mad metal,
thrashes against fiery footsteps.
It shifts across stark floor,
escaping enemy's armour.

We open frosted windows,
emitting sharp, cold air.
It chills us stone quiet,
huddled in our embrace.
My silhouette shrinks,
willing you to leave me,
to escape certain death.

I see your silhouette flow,
as light as the cold air.
It spins across the ground,
scattering frost everywhere.
An ethereal fog that breathes
in rhythm with your soul.
A shield of love protection,
away from anger's haunts.

A cold that snaps weapons,
shattering them across ground.
It freezes the enemy's anger,
cursing them with time's trap.
Dark souls frozen in winter,
bitten with pure aching white,
scattered into gentle snowfall,
that showers us with its love.

Stoic Solitude

Raw air abreath with white,
exhaling a fog upon vista.
In winter fall, I stand tall,
stoic amongst harsh blanc,
revelling in my solitude.

A silent snow blanket stares
deeply into my melted eyes,
exposing my absent heart.
It beats a river of raw tears,
that swarm my deep soul.

Ice's isolation preserves me,
fossilizing my stoic solitude.
No eyes to meet horizons
or words to fill the gaps.

Winter's fire burns within me,
hot coals sear the storm of days.
My eyes spark fierce flames,
simmering the sharp cold,
reviving its reclusive life.

In frost, the white burns magic,
shattering into tiny fragments.
Airy, light dots float freely
across the masked white sky.
Moments of my vivid life,
afloat like delicate snowflakes
across the smothering air.

My internal river runs madly,
drowning my hassled heart.
Battling its dark, sinking sadness,
it beats with brave determination.
One tumultuous time lingers,
its presence alluring in the fog.

Reaching out my shaking hand,
I cradle the moment in my palm,
witnessing its very wild nature ...

A raging, raw face swallows light,
pushing me outside in the dark.
The heavy weight of home echoes
as its door slams shut behind me.

Outside, alone in the stark white,
exhaling a deep, brave breath
across snow's blank canvas.

Harnessing my stoic solitude,
stepping my footprints of freedom
across the shining, pure white.

Wild Alive

Arms of crystal clear,
raised up to the dark.
Sans wings of wealth
that plague her heart.
A shade in moonlight,
fingers clawing rays.
Catching a light speck,
savouring its ways.

Foreign to her wild
is this cluster of light.
Sparking in her palm,
awakening her night.
Rising from the dirt,
her body thaws frost.
It is her hour to hunt
for a way back to life.

Swarmed by a bolt
of thunderous hooves.
A single ghost horse,
she once nursed alive.
The mare's eyes flash
like rays of lightening.
Her gaze strikes gates,
jolting them awake.

Mounting blazing back,
she rides the rageful mare.
Tearing through the gates,
shedding thunder on castle.
A tall, foreboding building,
with sinister, spiked turrets.
A single frosted window
bearing the breath of fog.

Pushing open glass pain,
she rides inside the room.
Hooves thrashing carpet
and stirring bodies awake.
Cries that shatter silence,
dark wings brushing by.

Wings that sting her skin,
burning cold with snow.
freezing her thawed torso,
setting her wild soul afire.
Trotting upon the mare
she sets a trail ablaze.
Fiery fumes engulf air,
exposing the dark wings.

A sinister creature lurks,
a body made of wax.
Its head a candle wick
aglow with sapphire eyes.
The cursed deep blue jewel
that took her mare's life.

Summoning her energy
she ignites a fiery furno.
The flame licks wick,
setting candle aflame.
Wax drips and drops,
burning creature alight.
A horrific scream
pierces eerie eve.
As the creature dissolves,
its wings set aflight.

Wings that return to her,
spanning across her back.
Reigning her as heiress
of her family's estate.
A rule that revives her,
kissed with breath of life.

She snatches the sapphires
as they fall through air.
They glow with vitality
in the palm of her hand.
Sapphires of deep sight,
returned to her mare.
A curse that is lifted,
her beloved horse is alive.

Hold onto My Fire Heart

Hold onto my fire heart,
kindling its wilful embers
in the glaring grey night.
Winter's chill has set in,
biting us with bitterness
and dousing our fire.

We are surged in a sea,
engulfed by age's anguish,
which crests and falls,
pulling us forcefully apart.
I cry out your name,
striking ocean's slander
with my wilful fists.

Submerged in sea's lair,
I thrash against terror,
fighting to burn bright.
Drowned by dark sea,
relinquished of my fire,
I am freezing like ice.

You are a bobbing buoy,
daring blue rock eyes,
meeting mine in the rage.
A stable soul in my chaos,
whose touch melts my ice.
My safe guide to submerge
and crawl upon coastal land
into your assured arms.

Your embrace is eternal,
dissipating the darkness,
in sync with the star shine.
Red-orange sparks radiate
from your stable soul,
granting me your love,
fuelling my heart afire.

A Shelter for the Soul

Across winter's icy plains,
blue lanterns are aglow.
Adrift and seeking a way
to relieve the chill of cold.

Shadows etch their life,
stretching across snow.
Life that I yearn to see
in lantern's guiding glow.

Like a tiny seed is light
that blossoms in shadow.
Abloom is its pure soul,
unearthed from the dark.

A gift of heat to plains,
as exotic as camp fire.
Lit shadow alleviates
the chill of winter white.

A gentle caress of heat,
strokes my tense skin.
My body shifts and sways,
dancing with live warmth.

A fire that tingles deeply,
alighting my longing soul.
A shelter I carry with me,
across winter's harsh cold.

Wild Love

She has eyes of smoky coal
that steam in winter's white.
Her gaze is hot with heat,
that lights candle aflame.
Gold specks dance in her eyes
as she stares deeply into mine.

Her hot flame melts the chill
as she draws me into her arms.
Her kiss a streak of lightening,
that electrifies my deep soul.
Undoing my shirt buttons,
she strokes my chest alight.
A pure glow that wraps her
in my deeply aroused desire.

Removing her scarlet cloak,
she bares her gorgeous body.
I am entranced by her beauty,
drawn to her sensual soul.
Her lips spark my skin
as she lowers me down.

On her scarlet cloak I lay,
staring up into her eyes.
They burn with intensity
as she straddles my body.
Bare naked and beautiful,
her coal steams her skin.
We begin to rise up high,
upon our scarlet carpet.

She scratches the sky hot,
as she circles her hips.
Mini flames burst alive,
sparking with our desire.
As she reaches her peak,
her cries set sky ablaze.
Allured by her wild love,
I revel in her raw fire.

Spirit of the Light

A dying age lies beyond
the fiery flames of night.
Black and barren ash,
void of human heart.

Winter's wrath hardens
the softness of my soul.
Standing tall in snow,
I face the dark life.

Arrows aching loss,
befall the blasted sky.
Scattering bare blood,
like rain upon my skin.

Dripping blood on snow,
I watch it pool and puddle.
Bathing me in bare life
of souls not forsaken.

I rise in black tatters
of soul lace that lingers,
gifting life from loss,
to my blood soaked skin.

A spirit of the light,
I set my voice upon night.
A falsetto freely soaring
across eve's evil blasts.

My lace lures the wind,
ripping away from my skin.
Abreeze in death's light,
it flutters its new feathers.

Piercing purple eyes
in dark dare to shine.
Black ravens born
from life's tragic loss.

Ravens that shine radiantly
with soul's white stars.
A prophecy of journey
across the dying age.

Bare feet across blood,
in company of close flock,
I follow the star trail,
across the plains of peril.

Free Soul

Iridescent bottle green leaves,
catching the snow drift of time.
Iced with wisdom's tender touch,
falling in piles across the land.

Leaves that whisper of dreams
that whistle their gifts in my heart.
Soft visions of life soaring freely
across these plains of peril.

Falling upon the red stains,
the leaves kiss remnant life.
My soul sobs in its mourning,
missing our departed lives.

In the raging roars of conflict,
flutter the tender leaf fall.
Silent messages of peace,
rippling through the firestorm.

In piles I lay and stare up high
at the beauty of leaf fall.
Gorgeous greens of growth
afloat in their longevity.

To gather such leaves together,
like the people I hold so dear.
To promise them due freedom
from the endless fight we face.

Rise of the Daffodil

Early riser, yellow and bright,
like the sun to warm our frost.
Awaken my soul to her song,
sweet new daffodil in bloom.

Allow my soul to be renewed,
healed by your radiant light.
Spark me with day's warmth
so I might uncurl my fog.

Sadness hued in dark grey,
like stormy clouds inside.
My walk heavy footed,
my heart aching for light.

I watch your petals circle,
spinning through the air.
Your stem reaches for me
and lifts me up so high.

Across weighted sky we float,
unveiling streaks of darkness.
Seeing her face fade in fog,
her mouth open in silence.

Capturing her song clearly,
through your corona.
Her words sung sweetly,
echoing across the air:

My sweet daughter, Ari,
a healer in new light.
Share your unique gift
and cherish all life.

A melody that soothes
the gloomy fog within.
My heart embracing her
tender and loving spirit.

My soul is at peace
as I say my final farewell.
Adrift across the air,
we erase the stark grey.

The dark begins to lift,
soothing my sad heart.
Winter is at its end,
my soul clear of its fog.

Kiss Me with Clear Sight

Roaring reds of night,
breathe fire on my soul.
Thaw my frozen heart,
kiss me with clear sight.

Kindle my will to fly
across the star galaxy.
Alight my deep cosmos
with zest for new life.

Uncloud winter's tears,
manifested in the dark.
Give it voice to speak
and shine among stars.

Star angel in snow,
blessed by my body.
Whisper away winter
and soothe my storm.

Gift to my soul starlight
to see through the rain.
Shimmer me with joy
that forgets the dark.

Out here in the open,
worries seem small.
I can fly the galaxy
and radiate new life.

I

Winter gale, you unfurl in such beauty,
like the wild orange tendrils of her hair.
Her eyes evoke deep passion with her stare,
as her spirit alights breeze's duty.
Wind, carry my boat across horizon,
that I might sail in her beauteous breeze.
Allow my very deep sorrow to unfreeze,
letting me lose myself with abandon.
Turn time wild so that it sheds my rainfall,
releasing the gale brewing my heart song.
Let her soft gaze scatter my love petals,
across hours in which we can still freefall.
United, our embrace may be lifelong,
wrapped warmly in the soul of her sepals.

II

Colour my heart with dappled shades of grey,
like the cobble stones I once stood upon.
Our home closes its door with volition,
leaving my soul adrift in disarray.
Pour storm's rain into my lonely body,
allow it to fill each narrow vessel.
Let my heart's saddened energy expel,
that I may feel that I am somebody.
Beneath my rainstorm, waves I will venture,
rediscovering my home in life's flow.
I search for a new place to rest my heart,
across unchartered earth of adventure.
May my soul shine with a radiant glow,
allowing my self love to never part.

III

Touch my heart with winter's breath of lifetime,
deep white fragmented within sigh's air.
A single snowflake is my love affair,
a symbol of his love and its sublime.
Raw and unique, he helped me discover,
myself aclimb the hilltops of darkness.
Recently, his voice became powerless,
within the dark he worked to uncover.
May he find peace within my history,
clawing his way through the irrelevant.
His hands might cup the face of my version
and help me ascend the truth of story.
May his snowflake always be brilliant,
rising us above the indecision.

IV

Cobble stones of my poor, artistic life,
grant me an avenue in the darkness.
A trail that lifts hunger's obsessiveness,
within my hidden soul's existing strife.
My voice is buried deep by winter's sleet,
empty of light's healing satiation.
On cobble, I feel anticipation,
to stand before new souls that I may meet.
Gift to me kind hearts within night's jet black,
who may be enamoured by my heart song.
I may be blessed to be granted harvest,
to help me survive winter's harsh attack.
May my voice lift the dark where I belong
and colour our care for starvation's test.

V

My deep roar resides in wild lion soul,
trapped within the slopes of statue fountain.
In my dreams I dare to claw at mountain,
ripping away the iron that plagues me whole.
Rain flow, gurgling within fountain's gate,
conjure up a storm to build up my fight.
Summon my wild nature, set it alight,
stream my fiery, brave soul and activate.
Ignite my energy across the plains,
chasing prey with paws of powerful speed.
Radiate my soul with burning sunlight,
allowing my roar to defeat dark rains.
My freedom will grant my life with new seed,
growing my power to guard with great might.

VI

Red moon, await the brew of night's blood flow,
coursing through your mesmerising body.
A secret soldier of dark's melody,
a burning rage within you as you grow.
In smoky haze of eve you breathe your life,
very afraid of ghosts of your dark past.
You hunt me down across winters that last,
forever in your burning, rageful strife.
You have faded light when I disappear,
a crescent moon who cannot chase my soul.
I haunt your existence across the cold,
challenging you to relinquish your fear.
You will realise that I am your ghoul,
a manifestation of rage so old.

VII

Warm fire, gather us in your raw embrace,
inflame our souls with sensual desire.
Rekindle our care for our love's own fire,
endow our relationship with good grace.
I have searched for the states of our desire,
yet they seem to be adrift in fire's kind.
I must ignore the ashes of my mind,
that have destroyed our once united wire.
O flame do give me confidence to be,
a woman who attunes herself to love.
It is my fear that dominates my mind,
freezing my soul so I cannot be free.
Firelight, please spark my deep desire above
any frozen doubts that do lurk behind.

VIII

Winter's quarter of fading white moonlight,
evanescence of our loving embrace.
We remain two shadows scattered in space,
lingering in lost love's narrowed eyesight.
If moonlight had a long, winding stairwell,
I would descend, staring into his eyes.
My heart's crimson roses would shed their lies,
scattering hope for our romance to dwell.
Persuaded, he may climb my soul's stairwell,
allured by my promises of love's ease.
Soaked so deeply with love's newfound rain drops,
he might surrender to his need to tell.
With love so pure, moonlight will always please,
uniting our tides above its stair tops.

About the Author

Susan Marshall is a novelist, fiction writer, poet, dramatist, essayist and the founder of Story Playscapes. She is also a theatre practitioner and an expert educator. Susan is highly skilled in working with young adults in theatrical, educational and community settings and is a recipient of a prestigious award for her outstanding and extensive work with young people.

Susan's love for the arts began in early childhood. She discovered she had a strong physical connection with her surroundings (her playscapes) and could work with moments of energetic motions, letting them breathe and take flight through writing and performance work. She has fond memories of her parents encouraging her to read and write stories. She would also decorate her backyard with sheets as curtains and invite her parents as audience members to share in her performance work.

Susan's first productions were in primary school, under the experienced guidance of her significant teachers: Kim Young and Stu Cooper. She portrayed the Narrator in the stage adaptation of Road Dahl's *James and the Giant Peach*. In her French studies, she also had the fortune to portray the King in the French stage adaptation of *Le Petit Prince* by Antoine de Saint-Exupéry.

In secondary school, Susan felt blessed to be taught English and Drama by Di Gagen, the professional Australian theatre critic and stage director. Di was instrumental in helping Susan to discover and harness her artistic nature and skills. Under Di's guidance, Susan learnt how to critique live theatrical performance and to further develop and refine her writing skills.

Di Gagen also trained Susan in the art of theatre direction, by allowing her to take on the role of Stage Director for the productions: *Just Equal* by Dennis Betts and *A Midsummer Night's Dream* by William Shakespeare. Susan also had the privilege of being taught the skills of professional pantomimic performance when she was cast as various roles, including Phoebe and a Field Mouse in A. A. Milne's *Toad of Toad Hall*, which was co-directed by Di and Steve Gagen at the Hartwell Players in Melbourne.

Di Gagen also introduced Susan to the world of St Martin's Youth Arts Centre in Melbourne. Susan spent many years there, further developing her skills in performance. She was privileged to be trained in the techniques of improvisation by the experienced Geoff Wallis and even participated in a number of *Theatresports* regional finals.

Another highlight for Susan at St Martin's Youth Arts Centre, was the opportunity to be trained by the professional actor, James Wardlaw, in Stanislavski's method acting techniques. Susan also worked closely with the highly esteemed Artistic Director, Brett Adam, on devising and writing the script for the production of *Orb.IT* for the Melbourne International Arts Festival. As an actor, Susan also enjoyed portraying various roles in the non-realistic production within the modern set design created by Darryl Cordell.

Susan attended La Trobe University, where she completed a Bachelor of Arts and majored in English and Theatre and Drama. In her English degree, she committed herself to learning to read, analyse and write a range of narrative types, from classical to post structuralist. Professor Richard Freadman was a significant lecturer for Susan, due to his encouragement of her reading and analysis skills in autobiographical texts; along with broadening her understandings of the notions of the self in writing and literary theory.

In her Theatre and Drama degree, Susan was fortunate to be taught the art of theatre performance and theory by the highly experienced and esteemed, late Geoffrey Milne. She was also blessed to learn from the amazing expertise of the theatre practitioners: Julian Meyrick, Peta Tait and Meredith Rogers.

At La Trobe University, Susan also enjoyed portraying various roles in the theatrical production: *As You Like It*, by William Shakespeare, directed by Meredith Rogers and performed at the Trades Hall in Melbourne. She also performed the protagonist in the post structuralist production of Virginia Baxter's *What Time is This House?* at the Melbourne Fringe Festival. Later, she performed Phrygenia in the production *Spartacus and Phrygenia*, (written and directed by Peter and Corinne at Créations Barquette Gitane), for the Banyule Festival in Melbourne.

Keen to learn more about theatre direction, Susan had the privilege of observing and being taught by the professional stage director, Richard Keown, as he directed the Australian premiere production of John Harrison's *Holidays* at Peridot Theatre in Melbourne. Later, Susan had the privilege of directing the Australian premiere production of Timothy Daly's *Beach: A Theatrical Fantasia* with a young cast.

Always passionate about the arts and wanting to share her knowledge with young people, Susan completed a postgraduate Bachelor of Education: Primary and Secondary, at Deakin University and was privileged to learn from the expertise of her amazing lecturers: Dr Jo O'Mara and Dr Jo Raphael.

Susan has taught professionally in primary and secondary schools for more than a decade and has undertaken the role of Head of Drama. She has also written a number of drama and literacy articles for academic publications and mentored pre-service and practising teachers. Susan has presented at state and national conferences in drama and literacy education, including at the Victorian College of the Arts, the University of Melbourne and at the Queensland University of Technology in Brisbane and has also worked as an executive committee member for Drama Victoria.

As time progressed, Susan immersed herself in the adventures of play writing with the intention of developing works for young adults to explore in the classroom or youth theatre settings. This led to the development of her play: *Broken World*, which was published by RMDesigned in 2013. The play was launched at the joint AATE/ALEA National Conference and positively reviewed by the Children's Book Council of Australia. RMDesigned also published Susan's second play, *Indigo's Haven* in 2016.

Susan has also written a range of publications, which have been published at Vocal Media in the U.S.A. These include, Susan's poems: *Grandpa Ben's Mysterious Notebook: A Tale; A Day Spent: the Playful Thoughts of a Tired Mind; My Nature Spirit: A Poem Celebrating my Connection with Nature; Is Summer Still Aglow Within Thy Heart?: The Eternal Shore of Summer Love; Winter's Breath: Mother Nature's Precious Time* and *Heart's Land*, along with her short stories: *Paper Jilu: A Journey of Her Notes; Gail's Red Horizon: A Fantastical Adventure; Hidden Magic: Part 1; Peonies for Masha: Her Journey Home* (shortlisted as a finalist in the Vocal+ Fiction Awards, 2022); *Stay; Tace's Lost Spirit: Searching for Vie* and *Bare Love: A Metaphysical Romance*.

Susan is an honoured recipient of the prestigious *Award for Special Civic Service*, which was presented to her by the Mayor of Richmond, Victoria, for her extensive civic contributions to the city of Richmond and the Richmond City Council. The Award particularly recognises her outstanding efforts in assisting young people through her work on the Richmond Youth Work Project and the Richmond Youth Council.

In 2020, Susan founded Story Playscapes, her writing and publishing business. It was here that she became globally renown for delving into her playscapes when developing her writing. Susan's written works are highly respected by a dedicated global audience.

As an author, theatre practitioner and educator, Susan brings a wealth of knowledge to Story Playscapes. She is passionate about empowering literacy development in her global readership. Susan is also big hearted in her discussions on social media, where she fosters a love for reading and discovery in her readers.

In 2022, Susan was privileged to collaborate with the world class designer, Ryan Marshall, on the book design of her debut novel: *Makeshift Girl: The Secret Heritage Trail*, which was initially published in 2023 and released across the globe.

In 2023, Susan continued her collaboration with Ryan Marshall and was honoured that he designed her play publications for young adults: *Fleur of Yesterday* and *All the Hope We Carry*. As the first two plays released in Susan's new Theatre Playscapes series, they officially present her monumental achievement: her new Theatre Playscapes theatrical style, developed for young performers, to readers and theatre makers around the world.

In 2024, Story Playscapes released Susan's novel: *Adira and the Dark Horse,* the first book for adults in the new Adira Cazon Literary Mystery series. Also released was Susan's exclusive collection of 30 poems for adults: *Bare Spirit: The Selected Poems of Susan Marshall.*

In 2025, Susan's magnificent collection of 31 poems: *Wild Soul: Contemporary Classical Winter Poetry,* is a tribute to her refined, globally renown, metaphysical artistry. Susan allures us into the wild presence, awakenings, emotions, journeys, manifestations, states and transformations of the soul with evocative, soul stirring personas, visual imagery and journeyed verses.

Acknowledgements

Outdoors, I immersed myself in the wild energies of winter (2024) in Melbourne. I was spiritually drawn to its mysterious, fierce and evocative beauty. The concept of the 'wild soul' flourished deep within me and was fleshed out in the creation of poetry in a variety of styles in this book.

The place of classical literary studies and their importance in providing foundations for true artistry, cannot be ignored. I am deeply thankful to writers such as: Emily Brontë, Anton Chekhov, Charles Dickens, Thomas Hardy, Ernst Theodor Amadeus Hoffmann, Francesco Petrarca, Edgar Allan Poe, Jean-Jacques Rousseau and Percy Bysshe Shelley, for their beautiful works, which have enriched my life since I was young. From such masterful writers, I have learned the artistry of using a range of classical styles, in order to create my own original stories and poetry.

Some of the poems in this book, such as *O Sweet Florence, Unearth my Soul,* are written as a tribute to the very special role that the city of Florence, its people and its history have played, in helping to awaken my true, wild soul and its artistry. Thank you so much.

Ryan Marshall is a deeply attuned and highly talented book designer. His work on this book is evocative and summons the 'wild soul' exceptionally. I am very privileged to collaborate with Ryan. Thank you.

Thank you to our global readership for their continued interest and support of my work. I am eternally grateful.

About the Book Designer

Ryan Marshall is a professional graphic designer, photographer and illustrator, with more than 20 years of experience in designing a broad range of monographs, trade and fiction publications for world-leading professionals in the arts, design, photographic, automotive, landscape design and architectural industries.

Ryan has applied his unique technical skill set to the design and creation of hundreds of titles and includes significant contributions to international bestselling publications and series.

Ryan has collaborated with Susan Marshall and designed Story Playscapes' publications: *Makeshift Girl: The Secret Heritage Trail, Fleur of Yesterday, All the Hope We Carry, Adira and the Dark Horse* and *Bare Spirit: The Selected Poems of Susan Marshall*. He is honoured to bring his highly proficient design and technical expertise to the book design of Susan's exclusive poetry collection for adults: *Wild Soul: Contemporary Classical Winter Poetry* by Susan Marshall.

About Story Playscapes

Story Playscapes, established in 2020, is an Australian, heritage trade publishing house, founded by Australian Author, Susan Marshall.

The business is dedicated to promoting positive approaches to literacy development. It nurtures a global readership by actively sharing Susan Marshall's diverse range of written works on its website and in professional publications.

In 2023, Story Playscapes released its premiere publication: *Makeshift Girl: The Secret Heritage Trail* by Susan Marshall. In the same year, Story Playscapes also released *Fleur of Yesterday and All the Hope We Carry*, the first two plays written by Susan Marshall in her exciting, monumental Theatre Playscapes series for young adults around the globe.

In 2024, Story Playscapes released the publications: *Adira and the Dark Horse* and *Bare Spirit: The Selected Poems of Susan Marshall*, by Susan Marshall, across the globe.

In 2025, Story Playscapes is honoured to release: *Wild Soul: Contemporary Classical Winter Poetry*, by Susan Marshall, a collection of 31 poems for adults that are a tribute to the author's refined, globally renown, metaphysical artistry. Susan allures us into the wild presence, awakenings, emotions, journeys, manifestations, states and transformations of the soul with evocative, soul stirring personas, visual imagery and journeyed verses.

Story Playscapes

DISCOVER THE STORY

🌐 www.storyplayscapes.com

📘 Facebook: /storyplayscapes

📷 Instagram: @storyplayscapes

www.ingramcontent.com/pod-product-compliance
Lightning Source LLC
Chambersburg PA
CBHW072024290426
44109CB00018B/2334